# SPACE SYSTEMS

# The Universe to Scale
## Similarities and Differences in Objects in Our Solar System

Fiona Young-Brown

Cavendish
Square

New York

Published in 2017 by Cavendish Square Publishing, LLC
243 5th Avenue, Suite 136, New York, NY 10016

Library of Congress Cataloging-in-Publication Data

Names: Young-Brown, Fiona.
Title: The universe to scale : similarities and differences in objects in our solar system / Fiona Young-Brown.
Description: New York : Cavendish Square Publishing, [2017] | Series:
Space systems | Includes bibliographical references and index.
Identifiers: LCCN 2016026965 (print) | LCCN 2016027456 (ebook) |
ISBN 9781502622891 (library bound) | ISBN 9781502622907 (ebook)
Subjects: LCSH: Solar system--Juvenile literature. | Planets--
Juvenile literature. | Astronomy--Juvenile literature.
Classification: LCC QB602 .Y68 2017 (print) | LCC QB602 (ebook) | DDC 523.2--dc23
LC record available at https://lccn.loc.gov/2016026965

Editorial Director: David McNamara
Editor: Caitlyn Miller
Copy Editor: Rebecca Rohan
Associate Art Director: Amy Greenan
Senior Designer: Alan Sliwinski
Production Coordinator: Karol Szymczuk
Photo Research: J8 Media

The photographs in this book are used by permission and through the courtesy of: Cover, p. 1 Victor Habbick Visions/
Science Photo Library/Getty Images; p. 4 Christos Georghiou/Shutterstock.com; p. 7 World Perspectives/The
Image Bank/Getty Images; p. 10 Bridgeman Images; p. 13 Archive Photos/Getty Images; p. 16, 26 Everett – Art/
Shutterstock.com; p. 18 Sheila Terry/Science Source; p. 23 File:Astronomical unit.png/Huritisho/Wikimedia
Commons; p. 29 NASA/Space Telescope Science Institute; p. 36 Photos.com/Thinkstock; p. 39, 43, 56, 71 NASA;
p. 48 Imagno/Hulton Archive/Getty Images; p. 53 Hulton Archive/Getty Images; p. 58 Comstock/Stockbyte/
Thinkstock; p. 65 Neil Armstrong/NASA; p. 75 NASA/JPL/STScI; p. 77 NASA/Johns Hopkins University Applied
Physics Laboratory/Southwest Research Institute; p. 79 NASA/JPL-Caltech/ESO/R. Hurt; p. 82 NASA/Crew
of STS-132; p. 84 NASA/JPL; p. 86 NASA/JPL-Caltech/MSSS; p. 88 Steven Hobbs/Stocktrek Images/Getty
Images; p. 95 Photo Researchers Inc./Science Source/Getty Images; p. 100 Vitoriano Junior/Shutterstock.com.

Printed in the United States of America

# Contents

**Earth and its neighboring planets
within our solar system**

# Introduction:
# The Mysteries
# of the Skies

If you look up at the sky tonight, when it is really dark, what can you see? If there are not too many clouds, then you will probably see lots of stars. But look more closely. You might see the **moon**. It might be full and round, or it might be just a thin sliver. Now, look back at the stars again. Do they all look the same? Do some look bigger? Do some look a different color? If you're lucky, you might even see some lights moving across the sky—the International Space Station.

At first, you might think that all of those stars up in the sky are the same. In fact, they are very different. If you watch every night, you'll notice that things never look quite the same. The moon will be a little larger or smaller. Some of what appear to be stars might have moved. So what's going on up there?

That is the question people have been asking for hundreds and hundreds of years. The earliest cavemen looked to the sky at night, waiting for the **sun** to come back the next day and wondering about the things they saw there. They quickly learned that the sky could tell them what time of day it was and the time of year. They knew that the sun would appear on one horizon in the morning and would work its way across the sky until it disappeared, only to return the next day. When the sun disappeared, the moon and the stars would take its place in the dark sky. The moon, too, would grow larger and smaller, disappearing completely for one or two nights in its monthly cycle. And, if you watched closely every night, you would learn that everything slowly shifted in the skies. This happened more slowly and guided us through the seasons of the year. A year, a month, a day. All were connected to what was happening in the sky.

What people didn't understand was why.

In time, people made up theories. The ancient Greeks and the Egyptians drew maps of the stars, noting how they changed. They realized that a few of the stars moved, so they differentiated between stars and **planets**. Some of the planets looked different that the others. Mars looked like a distant red glow, while Venus seemed to shine bright and steady. The planets were given names, and it was assumed that they all moved around us, as we lived here on a steady, nonmoving Earth.

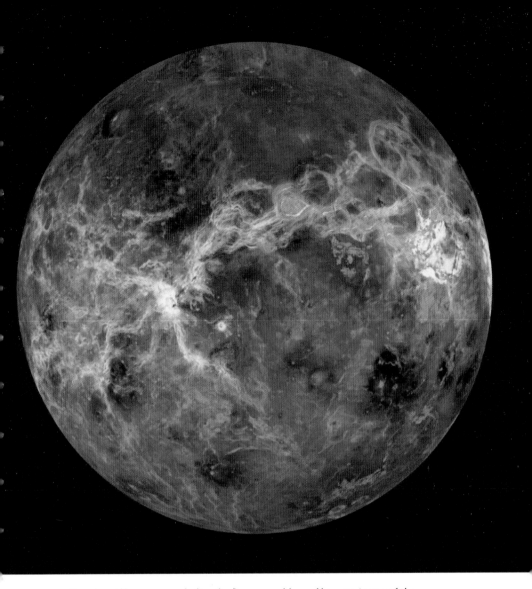

The planet Venus, named after the Roman goddess of beauty, is one of the brightest objects in our night sky.

Human curiosity continued. People drew more detailed maps and came up with more theories. New inventions came along that allowed closer examination of the moon and the planets. Mathematicians tried to find ways to calculate how far away the different objects were. At first, their calculations were very inaccurate. As technology has improved, so have the calculations. More planets were discovered; models changed. We seemed to live in a **solar system** of nine planets.

Now flash-forward to today. The days, the months, and the years are still the same, but what we know about the universe around us is very different. It is much bigger than any of us can imagine. And there is so much more out there. A man landing on the moon now seems a long time ago, but it was the beginning of many exciting new discoveries. Now, a few astronauts even live on a space station that goes around Earth.

Special **telescopes**, computers, and robots have traveled into space and to other planets. They have sent back pictures of fiery volcanoes, rocky landscapes, and gaseous clouds. Thanks to the pictures and other data, we know that different planets have very different landscapes, are different sizes, and move at different speeds. Some are surrounded by dozens of moons, while we have just one. Some are far too hot or too cold for us to live on, while ours is just right. We know that there are others millions of miles away. Could any of those be like Earth?

In this book, we will take a look at the planets and what we know about them. First we will look at what the ancient Greeks thought about the skies. We will learn how they named the planets and what we could tell about them simply by looking at them each night. Then we will look at some of the later scientists and inventors who realized that things did not work in the way we previously thought. They designed new models of the universe and helped to shape what we now know. In chapter 2, we will look at how these later astronomers developed scientific methods and tools to study the planets, and what discoveries they made. Chapter 3 will explore some of the people in detail. It will also look at NASA, an organization devoted to exploring and learning about space.

As our ideas about space and the planets change, so do the models we use to explain it. In chapter 4, we will explore the different models of our solar system. How have the models changed and why? What are the tools that we can use to make sure that our models are accurate? What new things are those tools teaching us?

Lastly, we will look forward. We have learned so much about the planets, but there is still much to explore. What comes next? Will we visit other planets? Perhaps live on them one day? What are some of the challenges facing us and what problems do we need to solve before living on Mars can become possible? And while we are searching for solutions to those problems, how is our knowledge helping us on Earth? How have our adventures in learning about the universe led to exciting changes in our everyday lives?

Prehistoric cave paintings, like this one in France, show the stars.

# Early Predictions

As far back as we can go in recorded history, people were watching the skies at night. Cave paintings in France, thought to be more than sixteen thousand years old, show some of the earliest star maps. These maps show images of the Summer Triangle and the Pleiades clusters. We can imagine the earliest humans looking up at the twinkling lights of the night sky and wondering what they were.

## EARLY OBSERVERS

Humans soon learned to use the motion of the moon and the sun to mark the passing of time. We still use these methods today. The sun brightened the eastern sky in the morning and traveled across the sky before disappearing on the other horizon. It would reappear hours later. This became the way of marking a day. People also watched the moon grow from a tiny sliver to a large globe before again shrinking and seeming to disappear. This whole passage of growing larger and then smaller marked a month. Ancient Egyptians, Chinese, Babylonians, and Greeks all recorded paintings of the stars and the planets. They were the earliest astronomers.

Some planets can be seen with the naked eye. In approximately 1000 BCE, Greek astronomers noticed that not everything in the night sky was the same. Some things stayed in the same spot and formed patterns; these were the stars and their constellations. But there were a few other things in the sky. They seemed brighter than the stars, and they seemed to be moving, wandering through space. Astronomers called them "planets," taken from the Greek word for wanderer. This led to a new question: why did stars stay still while wandering stars, or planets, moved?

One of the earliest recorded astronomers was the Greek Hipparchus. He was a mathematician, and he enjoyed watching weather patterns, but his keenest interest seems to have been studying the stars. In approximately 140 BCE, he produced what we think was the first detailed map of the sky. The map charted the visible constellations and planets. Some of Hipparchus's theories laid the groundwork for the next fifteen hundred years' worth of beliefs. For instance, he believed that Earth was at the center of the universe. He used his knowledge of mathematics to explain that the sun moved on a long path around Earth. This was what created the

The Greek astronomer Hipparchus drew what may be the first map of the stars in approximately 140 BCE.

seasons. He also tried to calculate how far the other planets were from Earth.

## NAMING THE PLANETS

We have mentioned that certain planets are visible to the naked eye. These are Mercury, Venus, Mars, Jupiter, and Saturn. We can't always see them, but at certain times, and if you know where to look, you can find them in the sky. The planets' names come from gods in Greek and Roman mythology. We don't know exactly who named many of them, but we can make guesses as to why they were named. For example, Mercury is the Roman god of thieving, travel, and commerce. Since the planet moves so quickly across the sky, it may have reminded early astronomers of a thief dashing from one place to the next. Venus is one the brightest objects in the sky and so named after the Roman goddess of beauty. When we see Mars, it looks like a red ball of fire, so naming it after a god of war seems appropriate. Even from millions of miles away here on Earth, Jupiter looks bigger than the other planets, so what better name than that given to the king of the gods? Saturn is perhaps the most difficult to explain; Saturn was the god of farming. Some believe that the planet was named after him to show the importance of agriculture to people.

Although Uranus, Neptune, and Pluto were not discovered until much later, this pattern of naming them after the gods continued. Neptune (the blue planet) is named after the god of the sea and Uranus for the ancient god of the heavens. Pluto is extremely far from the sun, and in constant darkness, so it is named for the god of the underworld.

## PTOLEMY

Hipparchus gave us a framework for looking at the stars and the planets, and Ptolemy further developed our understanding some two hundred years later. Ptolemy wrote the very first textbook about the stars and the planets. It listed more than one thousand known stars and their positions in the sky. Like most before him, Ptolemy believed that the universe was **geocentric**, meaning that Earth is at its center. He provided an explanation of why and where the planets moved.

According to Ptolemy's theories, Earth stood in place and did not move. The sun, the moon, and the five planets all moved around Earth. Yet there was a problem. Sometimes, it looked as though the planets were going faster or slower than usual; sometimes it even looked as if they were going backward. How could this be? Ptolemy found an explanation. Not only were the planets **orbiting** around Earth; they were also moving in their own smaller orbits. Each planet moved in its own small circular path within its larger path. This would explain why sometimes they seemed closer or farther away. These theories would go unchallenged for almost fifteen hundred years.

This seventeenth-century painting shows Ptolemy's geocentric idea of the universe, with Earth at the center.

Although Hipparchus and Ptolemy are considered the fathers of our understanding of the universe, not everyone believed their theories. Roughly one hundred years before Hipparchus produced his work, Aristarchus declared that, according to his calculations, Earth rotated on an axis and orbited the sun. This was the **heliocentric,** or sun-centered, model. It was ignored in favor of the geocentric one.

After Ptolemy, there were few developments in our understanding of the universe for quite some time. Persian astronomers made some interesting discoveries in the tenth century, but these went unnoticed in Europe, which was in the midst of the Dark Ages. Abd al-Rahman al-Sufi, known as al-Sufi, drew detailed maps of the stars. His work is particularly important because he is the first known person to have recorded objects outside of our own **galaxy**. He identified both the Large Magellanic Cloud (not "officially" discovered until the sixteenth century when explorer Magellan sailed around the world), and the Andromeda galaxy, which he called "a little cloud." A moon crater and an asteroid would later be named after al-Sufi.

## THE SIXTEENTH CENTURY

Our understanding of the universe grew from the sixteenth century on, thanks to such scientists as Copernicus and Galileo. Nicolaus Copernicus was a Polish physician and clergyman. His true passion, however, was studying the stars. Like Ptolemy and so many others before him, Copernicus was puzzled by the movement of the planets. Why did they seem to move backward at times? Everyone believed the geocentric model: Earth was at the center of the universe and everything else, the planets, the sun, the

Persian astronomer al-Sufi's detailed maps were the first to show objects outside our galaxy.

The Universe to Scale: Similarities and Differences in Objects in Our Solar System

moon, all traveled around it. How could Earth possibly be moving without us feeling it? As Copernicus tried to solve the riddle of why the planets moved the way they did, he started to think that perhaps Aristarchus was correct. Perhaps the sun was at the center of the universe, and we were moving around it.

Copernicus came to the conclusion that the planets were all traveling at different speeds. If planets passed each other at different speeds, it could look as though they were sometimes going backward across the sky. Furthermore, if Earth and all of the planets were traveling around the sun, and all at different speeds, sometimes Earth would catch up to a particular planet. Then it would seem like that planet was going in a different direction. This theory also explained the concept of a year—the amount of time it took Earth to travel once around the sun. Copernicus wrote his theories in a series of papers that made the church angry. Some believed that he would have been sent to prison, had he not died at around the time his book was published.

Many of Copernicus's theories could not be proven at the time that he was writing about them. That task was taken on sixty years later by an Italian scientist named Galileo Galilei. Galileo was the first person to use a telescope to observe the planets.

# Moon or Planet?

Earth has one moon, the basis for our calendar months. Some planets have many more. Jupiter has four famous moons (Io, Ganymede, Europa, and Callisto) but it currently has sixty-seven officially recognized, with more to possibly be discovered. Saturn also has more than sixty moons, while Venus has none. Some moons, such as Titan (which orbits Saturn) are even bigger than the planet Mercury.

So what is the difference between a planet and a moon?

The answer lies in what object the body moves around. If it moves around a star, it is a planet. In our solar system, the sun is a huge star at the center of everything. Therefore, Mercury, Earth, Venus, Mars, and the other bodies that orbit it are planets. On the other hand, if the body moves around one of these planets, it is a moon.

Just as our moon has giant craters and mountains on its surface, other moons in our solar system have interesting features. Some, especially around larger planets, are thought to be asteroids that got pulled into the planet's **gravity**. Jupiter's moon Io is covered in violent volcanoes and is surrounded by dangerous radiation. Another moon of Jupiter, Europa, is covered in ice, causing many scientists to think we could find life on it. There is just as much to learn about the different moons as there is still to discover about the planets.

# NEW INVENTIONS

A Dutchman, Hans Lippershey, was credited with inventing the telescope in 1608. Lippershey made eyeglasses. He realized that placing several lenses together would allow distant objects to seem much closer. Several other Dutchmen also tried to patent the device, each claiming the others had stolen his idea. Because it was so simple to make, no one was allowed to patent it.

By 1609, news of the telescope concept reached Italy. When Galileo heard about it, he decided to build his own. He then used it to look up to the skies. Many of the things he saw are things that we take for granted now. He was the very first person to see craters on the moon and the light of the Milky Way. Among his observations was the fact that Venus seemed to move through phases that were similar to those of the moon. At times it was bright and full; at others, it was just a small sliver. This proved to Galileo that the planets orbited the sun. He was able to show how, if Venus orbited Earth, we would only ever see a tiny portion of it because it would always be in shadow. Since it travels around the sun, the amount of light it reflects varies, and so it looks different based on its position in orbit.

Galileo didn't just learn about Venus. Using his telescope, he also discovered that there were four moons moving around Jupiter. So other planets could also have moons! Since then, scientists have discovered many more moons around Jupiter and around other planets.

While Galileo was marveling at moons around Jupiter and more stars than anyone knew existed, another scientist was exploring how the planets moved around the sun. Johannes Kepler was a German astronomer who had shown a keen interest in the stars from an early age. Copernicus had argued that the planets orbited the sun, but Kepler saw that this didn't explain the different patterns made by the movement of the planets. Kepler realized that the planets actually orbit the sun on an elliptical, or oval-shaped, path. This was known as Kepler's First Law of Planetary Motion. He proposed two more laws of motion. One determines the speed that each planet travels, and the other calculates the relationship between that speed and the size of the planet's path. With these three laws, Kepler could predict where a particular planet would be and when.

## CREATING A SCALE

Kepler was also one of the first mathematicians to help create the **astronomical unit (AU)**. An astronomical unit is the average distance between Earth and the sun. We now know that the distance changes depending where Earth is in its orbit. The average provides a helpful way to describe the distance between other planets by giving us a basic reference. Astronomers have been estimating the distance between the Earth and the sun for centuries. Kepler realized that Ptolemy's measurements were far too low. He calculated that the actual distance (or 1 AU) was 15 million miles (24 million kilometers). Later, scientists would estimate it to be 87 million miles (140 million km). Modern measurements, helped by computers and **satellites**, put the length of 1 AU at about 93 million miles (150 million km).

In 1596, Kepler had published a book supporting Copernicus's theory of a heliocentric universe. At the time,

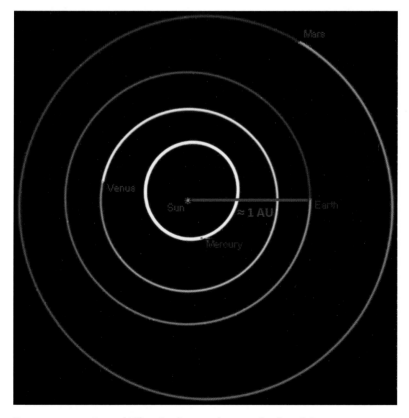

One astronomical unit (AU) is the distance between Earth and the sun.

he urged Galileo to publicly support the notion, but the Italian feared punishment by the Roman Catholic Church. Other scientists and philosophers risked being put to death if they argued against the Church's teachings. One of those teachings was that the universe revolved around Earth.

Later, Galileo became more confident about supporting the idea of movement around the sun. He became very interested in telescopes and experimented with building his own. His new tools helped him prove some of his theories. However, his discoveries were considered dangerous by the Church. He would face severe punishment for his ideas.

Galileo and Kepler had expanded our knowledge of planetary motion. Scientists now knew how the planets moved. What remained was to understand why they moved in such a fashion. The answer came in 1687 when English scientist Isaac Newton published his book *Philosophiae Naturalis Principia Mathematica*. Newton discovered that objects attracted each other with a force of attraction. That force was called gravity. The amount of gravitational pull between two objects depended on the mass of each object and the distance between them. Newton realized that this applied to the planets in orbit around the sun. The mass of the sun is so great that it exerts a gravitational force on each of the planets. That force is stronger for those closer to the sun. But the planets also pull on the sun with their own force, and the two forces pulling against each other is what creates the elliptical path. As they orbit closer to the sun, the stronger gravitational force causes them to move more quickly.

For thousands of years, people had been gazing up at the stars, wondering what they were, why some moved, and how they were all related to each other. The ancient Greeks had discovered the concept of planets, bodies that moved and behaved differently to the stars. By the end of the seventeenth century, our knowledge had grown in such a way that scientists could explain that everything in our galaxy revolved around the sun. They could also explain that each planet's motion was determined by its size and its distance from the sun. The foundations of understanding the universe had been put in place. As the following centuries would show, there was much more to be discovered in the sky.

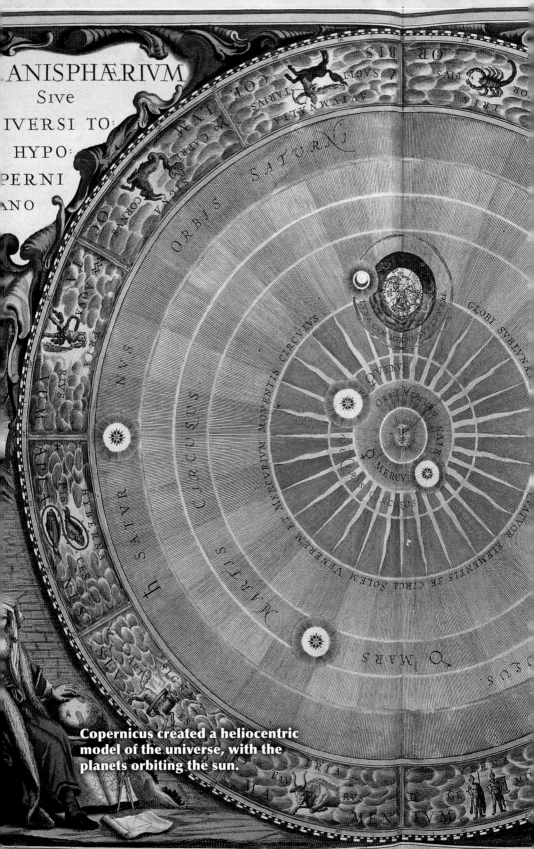

Copernicus created a heliocentric model of the universe, with the planets orbiting the sun.

# The Modern Understanding of the Planets

Our earliest understandings of the planets in our solar system and their relationships to each other were developed from three contributing factors:

- Observations with the naked eye
- Basic mathematical calculations
- The telescope

The third of these, the telescope, was not invented until the beginning of the seventeenth century. For the next few centuries, math and the telescope would continue to play crucial roles as scientists learned more about the universe. As the math became more advanced and the technology of the telescope improved, scientists could see farther and learn more.

In the mid-sixteenth century, Copernicus wrote his theories that the planets, including Earth, all orbited the sun at different speeds and from different distances. Some sixty years later, thanks to the invention of the telescope, Galileo observed Venus, saw details on the surface of Mars, discovered moons around Jupiter, and first saw the light of the Milky Way. He was able to confirm Copernicus's belief that the planets are heliocentric, revolving around the sun. Meanwhile, Galileo's contemporary, Johannes Kepler, was creating mathematical laws of motion that would chart the orbit path and speed of each planet.

Later in the same century, Isaac Newton would use math to develop an understanding of gravity. He showed how it influenced the orbit of planets, and how its force varied according to the size of the bodies pulling upon each other.

## DISCOVERING NEW PLANETS

Our understanding of the universe was growing, but there was much more to be learned. To start with, there were still three more planets to be discovered in our solar system, though one would be classified as such for only a short time.

### Discovering Uranus

Uranus was the first of these three to be discovered, thanks to a brother and sister duo of astronomers. William Herschel was born in Germany and followed his father's footsteps to become a musician in the army. Hating the life of a soldier, he fled to England to become a music teacher and pursue his interest in astronomy. His sister Caroline joined him there and soon shared his passion for the stars. She became the first woman to discover a comet. She would discover eight new comets in total. The pair is often credited with the foundation of modern astronomy. During their lives, they carefully mapped and cataloged more than ninety thousand stars. By this time, the telescope was an essential tool in any astronomer's kit. William taught himself how to make them, continually improving his skills so that he could create more powerful models.

Uranus was discovered by William Herschel in 1781.

# The Words of Galileo

In 1615, Galileo wrote in a letter to the Duchess of Tuscany:

*In my studies of astronomy and philosophy I hold this opinion about the universe, that the Sun remains fixed in the center of the circle of heavenly bodies, without changing its place; and the Earth, turning upon itself, moves round the Sun.*

It was a dangerous opinion to openly voice, since it was in opposition to the Church's belief that the universe revolved around Earth, and Galileo was aware that he might face prison time for sharing the beliefs that Copernicus had written about. In a 1597 letter to Kepler, he said:

*I accepted the Copernican position several years ago and discovered ... the causes of many natural effects which are doubtless inexplicable by the current theories. I have written up many reasons ... on the subject, but I have not dared until now to bring them into the open, being warned by the fortunes of Copernicus himself, our master, who procured for himself immortal fame among a few but stepped down among the great crowd ... only to be derided and dishonored. I would dare publish my thoughts if there were many like you; but since there are not, I shall forbear.*

In 1632, he warned the Church:

*You run the risk of eventually having to condemn as heretics those who would declare the earth to stand still and the sun to change position—eventually, I say, at such a time as it might be physically or logically proved that the earth moves and the sun stands still.*

One night in 1781, William was doing his usual observation of the stars. Suddenly, something unusual caught his eye. He spent the next few nights observing it before reaching the conclusion that what he saw was not a star. It was a planet. At first, Herschel wanted to name the planet after King George III, the reigning British monarch. Instead, it was decided that the planet should be called Uranus, after the Greek god of the sky. This fit with the naming pattern of the other planets.

After he discovered Uranus, William Herschel was appointed royal astronomer and Caroline was made his assistant. They spent the rest of their lives working as professional astronomers, charting and discovering comets, nebulae, and binary stars.

William was interested in studying the brightness of different objects in the night sky. Combining his observations through the telescope with Newton's law of gravity, he concluded that stars could also be in motion. He also attempted to map the Milky Way, named by the ancient Greeks because of its "milky" appearance.

## Discovering Neptune

The eighth planet to be discovered was Neptune. The discovery of this planet was different because it was the first to be discovered by math. Mars, Mercury, Venus, Saturn, and Jupiter can be seen at certain times without a telescope, and if you know where to look, you can find Uranus. Neptune is so far away from Earth than we can't see it with just our eyes. As it happens, Galileo had recorded Neptune through his telescope in 1612, but he didn't realize it was a planet. He thought it was just a star.

Once William Herschel has discovered Uranus, mathematicians and astronomers carefully followed its path around the sun. They soon noticed that something was wrong. Uranus didn't always move the way they expected it to. It was as if something else was out there, something large enough to exert a gravitational force that could affect the path of Uranus. Could there be another planet?

Two mathematicians calculated where they thought this new planet might be in the skies. They used what they knew about gravity and motion from both Newton and Kepler. In 1846, Johann Galle used their calculations to look through his telescope. There it was. An eighth planet. The planet was named Neptune after the Roman god of the seas. Just a few weeks later, astronomers discovered Neptune's largest moon, which was named Triton.

## Discovering Pluto

Astronomers watching disruptions to the path of Uranus decided there must be another planet. That led to the discovery of Neptune. In a similar way, those who started to watch Neptune were not satisfied. Percival Lowell was an amateur astronomer who built the Lowell Observatory in Arizona. He noticed that both Uranus and Neptune still seemed to wobble in their orbits. He was sure that there was another planet whose gravity was affecting them. He spent several years trying to pinpoint the location of this other planet, but he died in 1916, before he could make a discovery. In 1929, staff at the observatory decided to search again. In 1930, Clyde Tombaugh located the planet that would be called Pluto, after the Roman god of the underworld. Pluto was very difficult to locate for several reasons. Because it is so far from the sun, it is very dim in the sky, even when using an advanced telescope. It is also so far from Earth that it looks as though it is moving very slowly, almost too slowly to detect movement. Pluto takes 248 years to orbit the sun. Only by very careful observation and the measuring of the tiniest movements could Tombaugh tell that it was, in fact, in motion.

Pluto remained a planet for less than a century. As scientists learned more about the composition of the planets, they noticed something unusual. The planets closest to the sun are called **terrestrial planets**. Mercury, Venus, Earth, and Mars are all terrestrial planets. This means they are made of rock. Millions of years ago, the sun's gravity pulled pieces of rock towards it. Any gases that surrounded them were burned away by the sun's heat, and the clumps of rock joined together to form planets. Those farther away from the sun—Jupiter, Saturn, Uranus, and Neptune—never got close enough for their gases to burn away, so they didn't form solid rocks. They are known as gaseous giants.

So what about Pluto?

Its vast distance from the sun meant that scientists expected it would be a gaseous planet, like the others that are close to it. But in 1987, astronomers had a rare chance to study Pluto. It moved into a spot that only happens twice in its orbit, a spot that allowed scientists with their improved technology to take a closer look at the planet. They noticed that light was reflecting off its surface as it moved through this part of its orbit. This meant that it must be solid and not gaseous. They also noticed that Pluto's orbit didn't follow the same pattern as those of the other planets. Instead of keeping its own path, it crossed over Neptune's orbit. A few years later, scientists were able to find a huge area of space 9.3 billion miles from the sun. There they found other objects about the same size as Pluto. Could they all be planets? Was Pluto an object that was once in Neptune's orbit but which had somehow managed to escape its gravitational pull?

In 2006, the International Astronomical Union decided that there needed to be a better definition of a planet. Their guidelines state that a planet must

- Orbit the sun
- Be round or nearly round because of gravity

- Be big enough and have enough gravity that it has its own clear orbit

Clearly Pluto did not have its own clear orbit. It overlapped Neptune's orbit. Pluto was reclassified as a dwarf planet, meaning it

- Orbits the sun
- Is round
- Is not a moon or satellite of any other planet

Early astronomers relied on what they could see with their own eyes. Later, they used mathematical calculations and telescopes to study and discover new planets. One other useful tool that remains in use today is the **spectroscope**. Invented in 1814, the basic spectroscope combined a telescope with a prism to diffract the light. This allowed scientists to study the colors of the stars and planets in more detail. If we look up and study the stars closely, we can see that they are different colors. Some seem to be very white, while others may seem red. The same is true for planets. This is why Mars is known as the red planet. Once astronomers started using the spectroscope, they learned that stars were different colors because they were made up of different gases. What's more, the color and type of gas told them about the star's temperature and size.

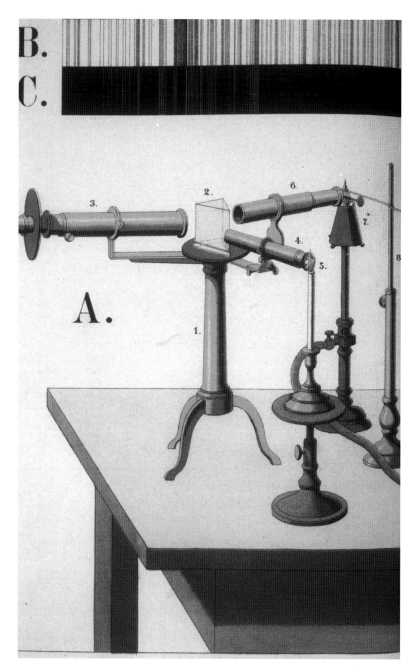

A spectroscope combines a telescope and a prism. It allows scientists to learn more about the gases around a planet.

Until relatively recently, humankind's study of space and the solar system was limited to observations or calculations that were made here on Earth. However, that would all soon change.

## A NEW AGE OF EXPLORATION

In 1957, the Russians launched *Sputnik 1*. It was the first man-made satellite to orbit Earth and took one hour and thirty-six minutes to do so. It remained in orbit for three months and transmitted radio signals strong enough to be picked up on Earth. The world had entered the space age. In January 1958, the United States sent our first satellite into orbit. Over the next decade, the United States and Russia were in constant competition. The first man and woman in space were both Russian. Russians also performed the first space walk and sent the first craft into space that would land on the moon and Venus. In 1969, America achieved a first when it sent the first men to the moon. The world watched as *Apollo 11* landed and Neil Armstrong became the first man to walk on the moon's surface.

Once people could send men and equipment into space, the ability to learn about the universe and the planets took a huge leap forward. Over the years, a number of **probes** have been sent into the skies, sending back a large amount of data. Some of these probes are designed to continually orbit one planet, gathering data about changes over time. Other probes have been sent as far out into space as they can go, never to return. Whether they have stayed in one part of our universe or journeyed into the unknown, they have all provided lots of new data.

## Studying Mars

As one of Earth's closest neighbors, Mars was the target for some of the earliest space probes. Astronomers already knew that Mars was smaller than Earth. Its diameter is about half the size of Earth, and therefore its gravity is much weaker. Mars had long been called the red planet because of its appearance. What else would probes teach us?

In 1877, Italian astronomer Giovanni Schiaparelli viewed Mars through his telescope. He noticed lines on the surface of the planet. He referred to them as *canali*, meaning "channels," but this was mistranslated as "canals." For decades this left some people convinced there were intelligent beings on the planet who had constructed such canals. They also assumed it meant there was water on Mars, despite evidence suggesting that Mars was far too cold to have any.

Nearly one hundred years after Schiaparelli's observations, in 1965, the Mariner 4 became the first probe to successfully pass Mars. Cameras took a number of photos of the Martian landscape. What they showed was very different to what people had imagined. The rocky craters showed no evidence of life. Clearer images, taken by Mariner 9 in 1971,

For a long time, people thought these markings on the surface of Mars might be proof of alien life.

showed a planet covered in volcanoes and canyons, with polar ice caps, evidence that water once flowed there. Five years later, Viking 1 landed on the planet's surface. Over the next six years, it sent back pictures and data revealing heavy radiation levels and a turbulent weather system. Since the

1990s, a number of robots or "rovers" have been sent to the surface. As well as taking photos, they have tracked weather patterns and analyzed soil samples in the event that humans can one day go there.

## Studying Venus

People often focus on Mars when thinking about space exploration and living on another planet, but the very first probe sent to another planet was actually sent to Earth's other closest neighbor—Venus. In 1962, the Mariner 2 probe flew past Venus. It confirmed that the temperatures in the planet's **atmosphere** were very hot. We now know that the surface temperatures are even hotter than those on Mercury. This is due to the dense atmosphere. These high temperatures made it difficult to send a space probe. The heat, combined with the atmospheric pressure, caused many probes to fail almost as soon as they entered the planet's orbit. A Russian probe was the first to land, in 1970, but within an hour, the heat and pressure were too much, and it stopped working. Twelve years later, another Russian probe was able to send the first images of Venus.

One key discovery about Venus is that its surface is covered with volcanoes and lava fields. Many of the volcanoes are thought to be still active, a way for the intense heat of the planet's core to escape. Several other discoveries make it different from the other planets in our solar system. For example, it does not create its own internal magnetic field. It has a very thin ozone layer (a thousand times thinner than that on Earth). Despite its extreme surface heat, there is a part of the planet's atmosphere that is colder than anything known on Earth. Lastly, it spins even slower than previously thought. One day on Venus is equivalent to 243 Earth days.

## Studying Mercury

The fourth terrestrial planet, Mercury, has been difficult to study in detail because of its proximity to the sun. Its surface temperatures reach 400° Celsius (752°F), although this is still less than Venus's 462°C (864°F). Mariner 10 flew past Mercury three times in the 1970s, giving us our first real images of the planet. Before this, scientists were not even sure what it looked like because the solar glare made it difficult to see through a telescope. The Messenger mission began in 2004 with the goal of exploring and learning more about Mercury, which is only slightly larger than our moon. Before the probe crashed into the planet's surface in 2015, it spent more than four years gathering and sending data about the surface. We learned that, despite its intense heat, night temperatures fall several hundred degrees below freezing. There are even signs of ice deep within some volcanic craters.

## The Gas Giants: Jupiter

The **gas giants** (Jupiter, Saturn, Uranus, and Neptune) have been the subject of a lot of study in the last few decades. Jupiter, the largest planet in our solar system, is five times as far from the sun as Earth is. Yet we can still see it because it is so big. It is eleven times bigger in diameter than Earth. All of the other planets in our solar system could fit inside Jupiter. Galileo and other early astronomers believed that Jupiter was a small sun because they could see moons orbiting it and assumed they were planets. This belief continued until the twentieth century when high-powered telescopes made it easier to study the faraway planet. Even though we know it is a planet, scientists say that it was almost a star. It gives off a lot of heat and its atmosphere is very similar to that of the sun: 90 percent hydrogen and 10 percent helium, with tiny traces of other substances. Researchers think it didn't quite create enough matter to continue the nuclear reactions that would complete its transformation into a star. That is what makes it so interesting to scientists now. They hope that by studying Jupiter, they can learn more about how the solar system was created.

Jupiter rotates more quickly than any other planet. One day is about ten Earth hours. Because it spins so quickly, it bulges at the equator. The planet also has a huge magnetic field because of its size and speed. This creates a strong belt of radiation around the planet. The radiation is so strong that it would kill any human who tried to pass through it. The radiation also means that sometimes the instruments on probes have difficulty gathering data as they pass through the belt.

Jupiter, Saturn, Uranus, and Neptune are known as the gas giants.

Despite the difficulties of radiation, space probes have
been able to give us a lot of data about Jupiter and its moons.
In the 1970s, two probes flew past. The photos they took
revealed that Jupiter has rings around it, rather like those
around Saturn. Later missions have revealed that the
largest moons around Jupiter each have their own distinct
atmosphere. Io is covered in active volcanoes, Europa is
covered in ice and is thought to have more water than Earth
does, and Ganymede is the only moon with its own internal
magnetic field. New missions hope to discover whether
Jupiter has a solid core.

## The Gas Giants: Saturn and Neptune

Like fellow gas giant Jupiter, Saturn has been found to be made up of 90 percent hydrogen. Also like Jupiter, it moves quite quickly, with one Saturn day the equivalent to just over ten Earth hours. The planet is best known for its rings. Although we now know that all four of the gas giants have rings around them, Saturn's remain the most visually striking. So what have we learned about Saturn that makes it stand out from the other gas giants?

For one thing, Saturn is the least dense planet in our solar system. Hydrogen and helium (the two main gases in its atmosphere) are the lightest gases and so, since it is smaller than Jupiter, it is the lightest planet. Being so light means it also has hardly any gravity. The rings around it are millions of tiny particles of ice, dust, and rock. Together, the rings are nearly 175,000 miles (281,635 km) wide. That's about three-quarters of the distance between Earth and the moon. But how do those particles in the rings stay in place if Saturn has so little gravity? Saturn has fifty-three moons and nine other satellites that orbit it. Those moons have their own gravity fields, which keep the rings in place. Saturn can be seen from Earth, but the probes that have traveled there have been able to teach us much more about the planet. For example, the largest moon, Titan, is similar to a terrestrial planet with a dense atmosphere and large bodies of liquid.

Of all the planets in our solar system, Uranus and Neptune may be the least explored, even less so than Mercury. Our one and only close-up look at Uranus was in 1986 when Voyager 2 flew past and spent five hours taking pictures. The spacecraft later passed by Neptune, in 1989. As a result, we still know very little about either. Uranus is the coldest planet since it doesn't have its own heat source, but there is some evidence of a boiling ocean on its surface. Uranus and Neptune are often referred to as the ice giants because of their cold temperatures. Perhaps the oddest thing that research has found is that Uranus's magnetic field is not aligned with the poles, as it is on Earth, Mercury, Jupiter, and Saturn. Instead, the poles on both Uranus and Neptune are close to the planets' equators. Meanwhile, the surface of Neptune may be very cold, but its core is very hot, hotter even than the surface of the sun. The hot core combined with the icy gaseous exterior results in a stormy atmosphere with incredibly strong winds.

## FARTHER INTO SPACE

Some of the same probes and telescopes that are telling us so much about the gas giants are also teaching us about planets and stars far beyond the limits of what we once imagined as the edge of space.

William Herschel attempted to map the Milky Way, showing how large our galaxy was and how many thousands of stars it contained. In the 1920s, Edwin Hubble went even further, proving that other galaxies existed beyond our own. He was assisted by other recent discoveries. For instance, just one decade earlier, an American astronomer named Henrietta Leavitt discovered the period-luminosity relationship, a way of using math to calculate how far a variable star is from Earth, based on its brightness and the length of time the star is most luminous. Hubble studied nebulae, clouds of dust in space that we now know are either where new stars are being formed or where old stars have decayed. At the time, no one was quite sure what they were. Hubble wanted to learn how far away they were. Using Leavitt's theory, he was able to calculate that the Andromeda nebula was much farther from Earth than the edge of the Milky Way was. In other words, there were stars outside of our Milky Way. Hubble was able to prove that there were countless galaxies outside our own known universe. Almost overnight, he changed modern thinking about the universe. Yet he was not finished with his astounding discoveries.

Hubble continued to study the different galaxies in far-off space, making note of their shapes. He noted that some, like our own Milky Way, are spiral with arms reaching from a flat center. Others are elliptical or oval shaped, with no arms. Still others are irregular. Hubble carefully measured the light that came from each one, using a spectrograph. He knew that the red end of the light spectrum meant that objects were moving away from us. The light from the galaxies he studied was shifting into the red end of the spectrum. The more he observed them, the more he realized that they were moving even farther away from our galaxy. And some were moving quite quickly. Not only were there other galaxies; those galaxies were moving away from our own. The universe was (and is) expanding. Eventually, he devised Hubble's Law, which states that the farther away the galaxy, the faster its speed. If one galaxy is three times as far from ours as another, it moves three times as fast.

Nicolaus Copernicus is often nicknamed "the father of modern astronomy."

# Scientists, Mathematicians, and Engineers

T he study of the planets in our solar system has always
been carried out by curious men and women who share
a passion for learning what is in the skies. Today, we take it
for granted that scientists, mathematicians, and engineers
have the support of various institutions—perhaps they work
with a space agency, such as NASA, or a university. Earlier
astronomers were not so fortunate. They often worked on
their own while they followed other careers, sometimes
working as teachers or as priests. Astronomy was their hobby
and their calling. If they were lucky, they might have a patron
who provided financial backing so that they could conduct
their research full time. In this chapter, we will look at some
of those early explorers, as well as the organizations behind
today's breakthroughs.

# COPERNICUS

One example of an early astronomer who made significant breakthroughs without much support is Nicolaus Copernicus. He is often called the "father of modern astronomy." The theories that he developed changed the way that we think about the solar system. His theories were also in direct conflict with the Church's teachings at the time.

Copernicus was born in 1473 in the Polish town of Torun. He was the youngest of four children, born into a wealthy and religious merchant family. When he was orphaned at the age of ten, he was sent to live with an uncle who was a clergyman so that he too could prepare for life in the Church. He entered the University of Krakow in 1491, and he spent the next three years studying math, astronomy, and philosophy. In 1496, Copernicus traveled to Italy to continue his education. This time, he studied religious law and medicine. While he lived in Bologna, he met Domenico Maria de Novara, a renowned astronomer. The two became friends and would often meet to talk about their studies. Chatting with de Novara helped Copernicus develop an interest in astronomy, and by the following year, he was charting the stars and studying the movement of the planets. He also continued his study of mathematics and was often asked to lecture on the topic at universities.

In 1506, Copernicus returned to Poland to work in the Catholic Church. However, he did not give up his pursuit of astronomy. Six years later, he wrote a small pamphlet claiming that the sun was at the center of the universe. The idea was very controversial at the time and was in direct opposition to what the church was teaching. Because of this, he published the pamphlet anonymously and shared it only with a few friends and colleagues. Even though the pamphlet did not have his name on it, word got out that these were his ideas. Religious leaders mocked him for believing that such a theory could be true. Copernicus decided that it would be better to focus more on his math, with astronomy as his hobby. He continued to read works by other astronomers.

By 1540, Copernicus decided it was time to make his ideas about the universe public. He began to write a book. In it, he claimed that the universe was heliocentric, that Earth rotated on its own axis, and that each planet had its own center of gravity. Sadly, he died a few days before the book was published in 1543, although some say that the book was placed in his hands as he lay in his sickbed. After the book was published, the Catholic Church immediately condemned it because it dared to say that Earth was not at the center of our solar system. The Lutheran Church also banned the book from 1616 to 1835. He may not have been able to prove many of his theories—after all, the telescope had not yet been invented—but the theories of Copernicus would strongly influence a later generation of astronomers, including Galileo and Kepler.

Copernicus may have theorized about the heliocentric nature of the solar system, but he had no way of proving his beliefs. There was no technology to help him. It was Galileo who was able to prove that Copernicus was correct.

## GALILEO

Galileo Galilei was born in 1564 in Pisa, Italy. For a while, he wanted to join the church as a priest, but his father, a renowned musician, wanted him to become a physician. He became a student at the University of Pisa but chose to study mathematics instead of medicine. Galileo went on to become a math professor. As well as working as a teacher, he completed a great deal of research in physics, helping to develop a modern understanding of both friction and motion. He also did some inventing and created a type of thermometer.

Galileo's introduction to astronomy came in 1609 when he read about a new Dutch creation: the telescope. He decided that he could build one of his own. While many scientists began to build their own telescopes, Galileo taught himself to grind lenses so that he could improve the design and create more powerful tools. The most powerful telescope he built was said to be capable of seeing things at 30x magnification. Soon he was observing the stars and the planets much more easily than he could without a telescope. In 1610, Galileo published the first results of his

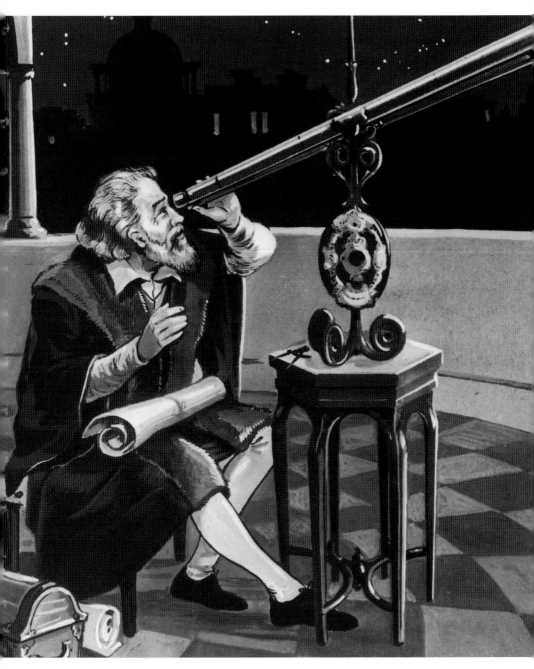

Italian astronomer Galileo built his own telescopes so that he could study the stars.

observations, which included four of Jupiter's moons and the "seas" on the moon. He also wrote about the phases of Venus, differences in lighting on the planet's surface caused by its movement around the sun. This discovery confirmed that the planets rotate around the sun.

Galileo's findings did not please the Church but they let him continue his studies, as long as he did not talk about his claims of Earth orbiting the sun. For a while, he continued to record his observations in peace. However, in 1632, he published a book with his evidence for a heliocentric model, supporting the theories of Copernicus. The book greatly angered the pope, and Galileo was put on trial for heresy. At his trial, he was forced to say that he was wrong about the planets. He was sent to prison for a while, before being placed under house arrest. For the rest of his life, Galileo was watched by the Church, and his writings were carefully censored. He died in 1642.

## KEPLER

While Galileo was building his telescopes and observing the skies from Italy, a fellow scientist was studying the orbit of Mars and creating the laws of motion that we still learn about today. Johannes Kepler was born in 1571 in Germany. Galileo came from an educated, fairly wealthy family, but Kepler's father was a soldier, most likely killed in combat when his son was about five. Kepler's mother was an innkeeper's daughter, so he spent much of his childhood helping at the inn. Despite the family's poverty, he did receive some education at a local school and then at a nearby seminary. He impressed his teachers with his natural intelligence and won a scholarship to study at the University of Tubingen. While there, he studied mathematics and astronomy. It was at university that he first learned about Copernicus. He seems to have instantly understood that Copernicus's theory of the heliocentric model was true. In 1596, Kepler, now a math teacher in Graz, wrote his first paper defending the Polish astronomer.

By now, Kepler and Galileo were writing to each other, sharing their research and opinions. Both knew that their ideas went against the Catholic Church's teachings, but Kepler may have found it a little easier to be public with his work since he was not a member of the Church. After Kepler published his paper in 1596, Galileo wrote to him that he did not dare make his own writings public because he knew they would be mocked. He wrote that if there were more people like Kepler, he would be willing to consider publishing his thoughts. For now, it was too dangerous to do so. Kepler wrote in reply, urging Galileo to think differently. He encouraged Galileo to "be of good cheer … and come out publicly." Kepler was certain that if the two of them made their theories public, the scientific truth would win. Mathematicians would have little choice but to agree with them.

The Kepler Space Observatory is named after Johannes Kepler. It launched into space in 2009.

Because of religious conflicts within the Lutheran church, Kepler was forced to leave his teaching position in Graz. He moved to Prague where he was able to work for a few years with Tycho Brahe, a well-known Danish astronomer. After Brahe died in 1601, Kepler took over his work. Using some of Brahe's research data, Kepler discovered that Mars did not orbit the sun in a perfect circle. Instead, it moved in an **ellipse**. He wrote about his observations and calculations in 1609, when he stated his first two laws of planetary motion. This is considered the first time someone documented what we call the scientific method—when someone asks a question, does research, makes observations, and then creates a theory based on that research.

In 1612, Kepler left Prague. His wife and children had recently died, and religious wars meant that Lutherans were no longer welcome in the city. He moved to Linz, a town in Austria. There, he continued his studies in astronomy, coming up with his third law of planetary motion and creating mathematical tables that could be used to calculate the position of a planet on any given date. Johannes Kepler died in 1630, but his work would influence Isaac Newton and many future scientists.

## Seeing Farther into the Sky

Researchers in the early seventeenth century relied on two primary tools for studying the planets: mathematical equations and the telescope. Telescopes have changed greatly since Galileo first read about Lippershey's invention and decided to make his own model. However, the basic design of the optical telescope remains the same. Today, hundreds of years after Galileo first used one to look at the details of the moon's surface, the telescope remains the most important tool for observing the universe. The first telescopes used two lenses to look at objects and, since scientists often learned how to build their own, they could make them to suit their own needs. By today's standards, Galileo's telescope provides blurry images, with not much range of vision, but when he used it in 1609, it allowed him to see things never before seen by anyone. Kepler also built his own telescopes. He used a different type of lens, which allowed a larger field of vision, but the image that he saw was upside-down.

It was Isaac Newton who introduced the use of a telescope with mirrors instead of lenses. This led to much

Huge telescope arrays allow us to see deep into space.

clearer images. Newton's version became known as the reflecting telescope. Those made with lenses are called refracting telescopes. Many of the telescopes in use today are reflecting ones, and some of the larger telescopes have many mirrors. The mirrors reflect more light, allowing researchers to see even farther into space. The telescopes used to look deep into space are huge, not at all like a handheld telescope. They are found at special research stations called observatories.

Other telescopes aren't even on Earth, but in space. The Hubble telescope was launched in 1990 and is one of the largest telescopes in orbit. Up above our atmosphere, there is no light pollution and no clouds to contend with, so the view of the stars and the planets is unobstructed. The Hubble telescope gathers data and sends it back to Earth where scientists can investigate. It remains in orbit around Earth, constantly taking pictures. So far, because of the amount of information it has provided researchers, NASA considers it "one of the most productive scientific instruments ever built." The Hubble telescope is about the length of a school bus. It weighs as much as two adult elephants.

## WILLIAM AND CAROLINE HERSCHEL

Another astronomer who built his own telescopes was William Herschel. In fact, he built more than four hundred different telescopes. Some were small handheld devices, but others were much larger as he tried to see more and in greater detail. The largest telescope he built was a 40-foot (12-meter) long reflecting telescope. Because it was so long, it was a little difficult to use. Most of the time Herschel preferred to use a 20-foot (6-meter) long telescope. However, the larger scope is what allowed him to spot two new moons around Saturn.

William Herschel and his sister Caroline were born in Germany in 1738 and 1750, respectively. Their father was an oboe player in a military band, and William followed in his musical footsteps. As a member of a military band, William traveled to and from England. Deciding that he did not wish to see any more wars, he chose to stay in England, even though this meant he would be accused of desertion from the army. Since he played multiple musical instruments, he worked as a composer, as a musician in various orchestras, and as a church organist. At this time, he showed little or no interest in astronomy.

Meanwhile, his sister Caroline came to live with him. As a child, Caroline had suffered from both smallpox and typhus. The diseases had disfigured her face and stunted her growth, so she never grew any taller than 4 feet, 3 inches (1.3 m). Her father told her that no one would ever marry her, so her mother decided her only choice would be to become a maid. In 1772, she joined William in England. She became his housekeeper and learned to sing and play the harpsichord.

She gave some performances and became quite well known, but since she would sing only when her brother conducted, as his interests changed, so did hers.

William Herschel was introduced to astronomy by a friend who was a violinist and mathematician. He bought a telescope but soon taught himself how to make his own. He learned to grind lenses and polish his own mirrors, and Caroline assisted him. Eventually, she would complete many calculations based on his observations. Both would go on to make discoveries of comets and nebulae, but it was William's discovery of Uranus in 1781 that gained them the most recognition. King George III made him the King's Astronomer, and he received many awards. Caroline also gained employment as his assistant. This was at a time when it was very unusual for women to work as something other than a maid. Both brother and sister would receive multiple medals for their scientific achievements. After William died in 1822, Caroline returned to Germany, where she died in 1848.

## HUBBLE

Probably the most famous telescope in space exploration is the Hubble telescope, which has orbited Earth since 1990. But who was the person that this telescope was named after, and how did he change our understanding of the universe?

Edwin Hubble was born in 1889 in Missouri. His father worked for an insurance company, and when Edwin was about ten years old, the family moved to Illinois, not far from Chicago. Edwin was a good student (although not in spelling), but he was most noted for his athletic abilities. While in school, he played football, baseball, and basketball; he ran track, and he broke the Illinois state high jump record. He attended the University of Chicago, where he played several different positions on the basketball team and helped win the team's first conference championship. After graduating from Chicago, he was awarded a Rhodes Scholarship to the University of Oxford in England and studied law there. At the University of Chicago, he had worked as a lab assistant to one of his physics professors. Some historians believe this was because of his interest in astronomy and that he only studied law to please his father.

In 1913, Hubble's father died. Edwin returned from Oxford to care for the family, now living in Louisville, Kentucky. He taught physics and math and coached basketball for a year, but he decided to go back to university to study astronomy. As soon as he finished his PhD, World War I broke out; Hubble enlisted in the military. He served in the army throughout the war, although he never actually saw any combat. After the war and a year of study in Cambridge, Hubble took a position at the Mount Wilson Observatory in Pasadena, California. He worked there from 1919 until his death in 1953. During his time at Mount Wilson, Hubble proved not only that other galaxies existed, but also that the universe is constantly expanding. His discoveries forever changed what we know about astronomy. Edwin Hubble had set out to map the entire universe. The telescope that bears his name continues that work today.

## NASA

For many of the earliest astronomers such as Copernicus and Galileo, studying the skies was a hobby, or something that they were only able to do with the support of a wealthy patron. William Herschel was able to make a living as an astronomer thanks to his discovery of Uranus and the resulting position as the King's Astronomer. Some later scientists would work at universities, where they could also do research.

Nowadays, there are a number of very important organizations that work with some universities and independently to support space research. The organizations bring together all sorts of scientists, mathematicians, and engineers to collaborate on projects. Together they have sent men to the moon and probes into the deepest reaches of space. The most famous of these organizations is the National Aeronautics and Space Administration, or NASA.

NASA was created in October 1958 "to provide for research into the problems of flight within and outside the Earth's atmosphere, and for other purposes." Its origins can be traced back to events from a decade earlier. After

World War II, both America and the Soviet Union had been pushing the boundaries of science, experimenting with hydrogen-fueled weapons and rockets. The two countries were opposed on many subjects, including politics and world security. Each attempted to beat the other in the development of weapons (the hydrogen bomb) and then in the "space race," as a way of proving that they were better than the other. Both countries announced plans to build a satellite to collect scientific data about Earth.

In 1957, the Soviet Union launched *Sputnik 1*. It was the world's first satellite. A few months later, *Explorer 1* would become the United States' first satellite. NASA was created as a nonmilitary American organization devoted to space exploration. In the beginning, there were three research laboratories, in Virginia, Ohio, and California. Facilities in Maryland and Alabama soon were added, and now there are ten NASA research centers around the country.

In the first decade after NASA's launch, both the United States and the Soviet Union launched multiple satellites and then human space flights, each country racing to beat the other to the next research milestone. In 1961, Alan Shepard became the first American in space, and in 1962, John Glenn was the first American to orbit Earth. Additional missions were focused on one goal: landing a man on the moon. President John F. Kennedy had said in 1961 that by the end of the decade, NASA should be able to land a man on the

*Apollo 11* landed on the moon in 1969. Here, astronaut Buzz Aldrin is standing outside the lunar module.

# The Lunar Lander

The Smithsonian National Air and Space Museum in Washington, DC, features all sorts of interesting vehicles and technology that have been used to explore the planets and stars. One set of items comes from the very first time an astronaut set foot on soil that was not on Earth. The museum has four hundred different objects that are linked to the Apollo 11 mission, the first to land on the moon. Some of these objects are small, everyday items that are needed even in space—a basic medical kit, scissors, and a watch, for example. Then there are more specialized pieces of equipment, such as containers for carrying soil samples, camera equipment, and oxygen masks. The clothing worn by the astronauts is also on display, so visitors can see the space suit worn by Buzz Aldrin and the headset worn by Neil Armstrong, as well as helmets and gloves.

Then there are the larger items on display. The command module of *Apollo 11* served as the living quarters for the three astronauts during their mission to the moon. They worked, ate, and slept there. It was the only part of the larger spacecraft to return to Earth and has been at the museum since 1970. Another part of the spacecraft was the lunar module and you can see one on display at the Air and Space Museum (though it's not from the moon mission). Twelve lunar landing modules were built for the Apollo missions. The one displayed was expected to go into space on a test mission, but since the first test went so well, the second was canceled. As for the original *Apollo 11* lunar module, it's still on the moon.

moon and bring him home again safely. The race was heating up. On July 20, 1969, the United States, thanks to NASA, won that key stage of the space race. *Apollo 11* landed on the moon and Neil Armstrong became the first man in history to take a step on the lunar landscape. Today, we all know his famous words: "That's one small step for man, one giant leap for mankind." Armstrong and fellow astronaut Buzz Aldrin took some photos and soil samples before returning to Earth. Several more NASA missions traveled to the moon to collect data, with the program ending in 1972 after the Apollo 17 mission.

Space flights resumed in the 1980s, thanks to the development of the space shuttle, which was designed to be used multiple times. The shuttles allowed for a crew of two to eight people to be in space for as long as seventeen days. By 1995, Russian and American astronauts were working together (the two countries had briefly conducted a joint research program in 1975) when the shuttle docked at the Mir Space Station. During the thirty-year space shuttle program, more than three hundred astronauts went into space on a total of 135 missions. The final shuttle, *Atlantis*, landed in 2011.

NASA's attention then turned to the construction of the International Space Station. The ISS is a joint project between NASA, the Russian Federal Space Agency (RKA), the European Space Agency (ESA), the Japan Aerospace

Exploration Agency (JAXA), and the Canadian Space Agency (CSA). Astronauts can spend longer periods of time living in space (typically six months) while they conduct research and collect data.

NASA has also been continuing important, unmanned space missions. These include satellites that orbit Earth, rovers that have explored the surface of Mars, and probes that have traveled to Uranus, Neptune, and beyond.

## ESA

While the space race was a rivalry between the Soviet Union and the United States, other nations have been interested in space exploration as well, as demonstrated by those involved with the International Space Station. One such organization that has added to our understanding of the universe and the planets is the European Space Agency (ESA). The ESA was created in 1975 and is a collaboration between twenty-two member countries. Its main centers are in the Netherlands, Germany, Italy, Norway, and Spain. Many of the ESA's missions have been conducted jointly with NASA. For example, in 1978, the two teamed up for the International Ultraviolet Explorer (IUE). The IUE is a high-orbit telescope that was the first to be operated in real time by scientists on Earth. In the late 1980s, ESA started sending its first probes into deep space to map the stars and to study comets.

Planned future missions include those designed to study Mercury and Jupiter, as well as those designed to map Earth's gravity, wind patterns, and vegetation change.

The imagination of these scientists, from the early stargazers to modern research organizations with the newest technology, has helped to shape our knowledge of the solar system.

**The planets of our solar system**

# Visualizing the Universe

T he earliest stargazers in ancient Greece, Egypt, and
elsewhere believed that we lived in a geocentric or Earth-
centered universe, where the sun, moon, and stars were
in constant rotation around an unmoving Earth. Later,
Copernicus theorized otherwise—that we were, in fact,
all orbiting the sun. A very controversial idea when first
proposed, this theory was eventually proven to be correct. The
heliocentric, or sun-centered, model was understood to be the
accurate model of our solar system. Both models differed in
terms of what was at the center of the rotation paths (Earth
or the sun), but they were similar in that they both were
based on the knowledge of orbits and constant rotation. The
moon revolves around Earth; Earth rotates on its own axis;
and Earth and other planets revolve around the sun.

We base measurements of time upon the patterns of rotation. One day is the amount of time Earth takes to rotate on its axis. One month is the amount of time for the moon to circle Earth. One year is the amount of time it takes for Earth to complete its orbit path around the sun. As we learned more about other planets, we learned that some had longer orbit paths because they were farther away from the sun. Others that were closer had shorter, quicker orbits.

Our understanding of orbits went a long way in helping astronomers discover some of the planets in our solar system. To learn more, we had to gain knowledge in other areas. This knowledge would be combined to help us create early models of the universe. Some planets could be seen with the naked eye, and then more easily through a telescope. But others needed the benefit of further learning before they could be discovered. We couldn't find them until we knew about gravity, orbits, and more.

Uranus was discovered by William Herschel, thanks to a telescope and the understanding that, as a planet, it moved across the sky on a certain path. But Neptune was discovered thanks to mathematics and our knowledge of gravity. The more scientists learned, the more they were able to notice problems or anomalies. So, when they noticed that Uranus seemed to be pulled in an unexpected direction, they were able to theorize that there must be something else out there, capable of exerting a noticeable gravitational field. Newton's laws of gravity, Kepler's laws of planetary motion, and some careful calculations enabled mathematicians to pinpoint where in the sky they might find this mysterious gravitational field. Sure enough, they found Neptune.

The discovery of Uranus had led to the discovery of Neptune. Then came the discovery of Pluto. Again, this was the result of one astronomer studying the skies, noticing something that he couldn't explain, and calculating what and where it might be.

But all of this took time. Before the invention of computers, scientists could only deduce the existence of planets and plot their orbits based on the effect that they had on the environment around them. So when one planet's orbit seemed to vary from what was expected, they could focus on that area of the solar system to seek the source of the anomaly. Sometimes this took decades, especially when the planets were so far away and took such a long time to rotate around the sun. Neptune takes nearly 165 years to orbit the sun. One astronomer might note an anomaly, but it might be decades before the planet is in that same position again. It would fall to another astronomer to complete the research years later, watching to see if that same anomaly might repeat.

Fortunately, astronomers now have more technologically advanced tools available. Modern tools allow them to create a variety of models and investigate those models in a much shorter timespan than in previous centuries. Computers have played an important role in allowing us to discover and model the universe. And as the distances probes explore become ever greater and the calculations ever more complex, so the need for more advanced computers is essential.

## COMPUTER MODELS

Computers have also made it possible to create accurate scale models of the solar system. Earlier sketches of the planets, whether it was the geocentric or the heliocentric model, all showed objects of a similar size revolving around another similar-sized object. They all moved in perfect circles, all a similar distance apart. Of course, we now know that those models are not accurate. The sizes of the planets differ enormously, as do the distances between their orbital paths. Furthermore, those orbital paths are not perfect circles but elliptical. If you were to try to draw a scale model of the solar system on a piece of paper, most planets would be too small to see because the distances between them are so great.

Now consider most images you've seen of our solar system. The planets are generally lined up in order of their nearness to the sun, all on the same plane, with none truly above or below the others. Is that really how the planets orbit the sun? Does it really look like a flat disk? The answer is yes. The orbits of most of the planets in our solar system are roughly in line with the equator of the sun!

Saturn is easily recognized by the rings of ice, debris, and dust that surround it.

This means that all of the planets in our solar system act like the rings of Saturn. They form a wide belt around the middle of the sun. This is not the case for all solar systems that scientists have observed, though. Some faraway solar systems have planets that orbit their sun in orbits far from that sun's equator. That kind of orbit would make a model of that solar system more like a sphere than the disk-like shape of our own solar system.

# DISCOVERING AND CHANGING DEFINITIONS

As the tools available to observe and study the objects in space continue to improve, so does our understanding of the universe around us. Some long-held beliefs are changed as new evidence becomes available. Much like Copernicus changed our view of the solar system from geocentric to heliocentric, our understanding of other "facts" about our solar system has changed. Take Pluto, for example. For decades after it was discovered, Pluto was considered to be the ninth and final planet in our solar system. However, the International Astronomer's Union (the group that sets the guidelines for describing objects in space) struggled for many years on the question of whether Pluto is a planet.

Why was this a question? Because as scientists learned more about the solar system, they discovered that Pluto was not as unique as they thought. In 1978, Pluto's moon Charon was discovered. Charon is almost half the size of Pluto. When scientists used it to determine the mass of Pluto, the planet was much smaller than they originally thought.

Pluto's position as the ninth planet was finally removed after the discovery of Eris in 2005. Lying far outside of the traditional solar system, Eris takes 557 years to complete one orbit of the sun. Using the Hubble space telescope and the Keck observatory, scientists compared the size of Eris to the size of its small moon, Dysnomia. This allowed them to

As of 2006, Pluto has been considered a dwarf planet.

estimate the size of Eris. To their surprise, Eris was larger than Pluto.

This discovery rocked the astrological world. It forced the International Astronomer's Union to re-examine their definition of a planet. In 2006, the IAU announced that Pluto, Eris, and another similarly sized astral body in our solar system, Ceres, would all be given the classification of "dwarf planet."

## NEW PLANETS?

Improved tools for observation such as space-based telescopes and advanced computer modeling don't just lead to changes in the things we already know. They also lead to new discoveries. Remember that Pluto was discovered in 1930 when astronomers were looking for a ninth planet due to strange patterns they observed with the orbit of Neptune. These patterns suggested a gas giant similar in size to Neptune must be out there. Pluto was discovered. However, it was much smaller than even Earth's moon. It was definitely not the gas giant that early calculations suggested must be out there.

Some astronomers decided to continue looking for that mysterious gas giant. Luckily, the New Horizons Space Probe passed Pluto in 2015. Using advanced computer models and the detailed data that the probe sent back, they found evidence to support their theory that there is a ninth

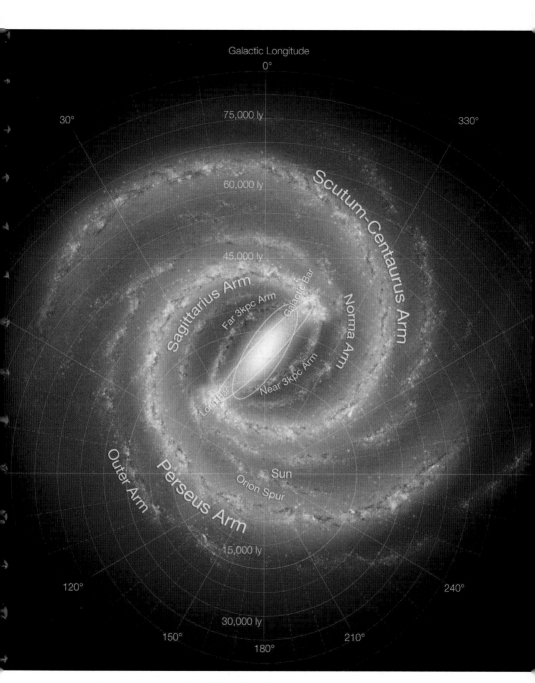

Galactic Longitude
0°

75,000 ly

30°                                                330°

60,000 ly

Scutum-Centaurus Arm

45,000 ly

Sagittarius Arm

Far 3kpc Arm     Galactic Bar

Norma Arm

Long Bar     Near 3kpc Arm

Outer Arm     Perseus Arm

Sun

Orion Spur

15,000 ly

120°                                                240°

30,000 ly

150°          180°          210°

An artist's impression of the Milky Way, showing spiral arms

# The International Space Station

Circling Earth every ninety minutes is the International Space Station (ISS). The ISS is a complex structure that is our only inhabited outpost in space. People live, work, and sleep there. Five space agencies and fifteen countries joined together to create the ISS. It was even built in space as it orbited Earth, starting with a Russian module in 1998. More modules, laboratories, living spaces, and solar panels were added. Since November 2000, there has always been someone living on the space station. Since 2009, there has typically been a six-person crew on board. The ISS is now being adapted to include docking space for the first commercial spacecraft.

Crew members on the ISS carry out research in lots of different areas, including the effects of weightlessness on health, communications in space, and taking images of Earth (which can track natural disasters and effects of climate change). Scientists have computer models for how they think things work in space, but people can do experiments to prove whether those models are right or wrong. Some of their research can benefit us on Earth. For example, one experiment helped to reveal changes in the human immune system that might be able to help doctors predict certain illnesses in the future. Other experiments might teach us how to grow food in space.

If you know where to look, you can see the ISS crossing the sky as it orbits the Earth. So if you see what looks like a star moving across the horizon, there could be people looking down at you.

planet, far beyond the orbit of Pluto. It has been nicknamed Planet X. The mysterious Planet X is believed to have an orbit so large that it takes it somewhere between ten thousand and twenty thousand years to complete one trip around the sun. That means it takes Planet X over forty times longer than it takes the former ninth planet, Pluto, to make the same trip. Its existence has not been proven yet. Astronomers are now working to find out if there really is a Planet X, or if there is some other phenomenon out there causing the abnormalities that have been observed.

Of course, new discoveries are not limited to objects within our solar system. In 2009, NASA launched the Kepler space telescope. Unlike the Hubble telescope, which has a broad mission for space observation, the Kepler telescope's job was very specific. It was intended to look at a specific star field in one region of space. Through observation, it will identify **exoplanets**. An exoplanet meets the International Astronomer's Union definition of a planet, but it orbits a different sun than the one at the center of our solar system. The Kepler telescope provided an incredible amount of data to scientists over the course of its six-year mission. In fact, it sent back so much data that, even with modern computer technology, scientists will be analyzing that data for years to come.

As of May 2016, NASA announced that the Kepler space telescope's planetary catalog contained 4,302 objects

The International Space Station has been orbiting Earth since 1998 and can house six astronauts.

that could be potential planets. NASA scientists have done intensive study of the objects. They believe that 1,284 of these objects meet all the criteria of being classified as a planet with 99 percent certainty. This is the largest verified discovery of exoplanets to date. Now scientists will take the next step. Nine of these new planets have been found in a so-called "habitable zone" of space. This is an area where the planetary temperatures might make it possible for liquid water to exist. Scientists will carefully study these nine planets. Including these nine new potential life-bearing worlds, scientists have discovered twenty-one planets that have conditions capable of supporting life as we currently understand it.

Don't pack your bags for the trip to a "New Earth" just yet. The nearest one of these planets found is about thirteen light years away. That might not sound very far in terms of the size of our entire galaxy. But one light year (the distance light can travel in one year) is about 6 trillion miles (or about 10 trillion km). It is clear we won't be traveling there anytime soon. However, remember that at the time of Copernicus, it took a ship over three months to journey to the "new world" from Europe. Now we make that trip in less than a day. Technological advances have made the earth a relatively smaller place in the past few hundred years. Perhaps, as our advances continue, the scale of the universe will seem a little smaller. If it does, maybe one day we will see one of these new worlds with our own eyes.

Space probes can travel deep into space, sending back images and data to teach us more about faraway planets.

# The Universe Today and Tomorrow

5

S pace probes and telescopes have sent us a lot of data. That data has allowed scientists to learn a great deal about the universe and the planets in our solar system. Thanks to space probes, we know about the temperatures, atmospheres, and gravitational fields of the different planets. We have been able to study soil samples from some and explore the landscapes of others thanks to hundreds of photographs. The data provided by probes has changed how we think of space.

They have also made fascinating new discoveries. Probes that have gone deep into space have indicated the existence of other planets—not just one or two, but thousands! This leaves scientists with many exciting questions to explore and answer. Is there really a Planet X at the edges of our solar system? Do some of these newly discovered exoplanets offer the potential for life? And of course, there are still questions to be answered closer to Earth. Could we one day live on the moon? Or on Mars? Will the things we see in science fiction movies one day become our reality?

## PROBES

Probes have been a useful way to explore the universe for many reasons, not just because of the amount of data they can

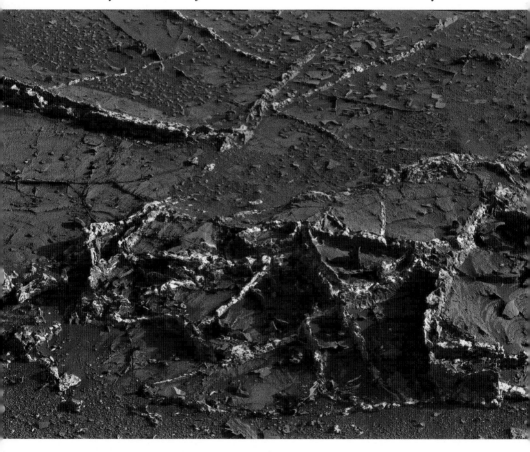

The surface of Mars is rich with minerals.

The Universe to Scale: Similarities and Differences in Objects in Our Solar System

collect. They are cheaper than manned space missions, and safer, since they do not carry a crew. They can travel extreme distances and enter environments that humans could not survive. If the mission does fail, the loss of a robot or a probe is much less disastrous than the loss of a human crew.

But there are still challenges to sending a probe into space. Although cheaper than a manned mission, a probe can still cost millions of dollars. The Kepler mission cost $550 million. Then there are challenges facing power. The Mars rover vehicles have used radioisotopes or nuclear power supplies, sometimes combined with solar panels. Nuclear power is also used in deep space probes. That far from the sun, solar panels are of no use. As we search even deeper into space, we will need power sources capable of lasting even longer.

## TRAVELING TO ANOTHER PLANET

Probes and the data they gather are very exciting, but the next step in space exploration is manned flight. People have been to the moon and the International Space Station. Some scientists believe that we might soon be able to travel to other planets. Commercial businesses have already built and are testing their own craft, which are designed to take people to the International Space Station and to the lower reaches of Earth's orbit. They are in the testing stage.

Earth is overcrowded; resources are becoming scarcer and climate change more severe. Building colonies on the moon or other planets looks more attractive. There are lots of natural resources out there waiting to be uncovered: minerals and water.

Is a colony on Mars possible? It might look like this.

The Universe to Scale: Similarities and Differences in Objects in Our Solar System

Mars is the most likely planet for a new colony. It is relatively close to Earth and is rich in minerals. The minerals don't even need to be mined because they are readily available on the ground and can simply be scooped up. Researchers are also keen to continue searching there for some indication of life, most likely as tiny microbes or bacteria. Creating such a colony, on Mars or elsewhere, will be far from easy.

## CHALLENGES TO VISITING OTHER PLANETS

Some of the challenges facing such exploration are similar to those difficulties already mentioned with space probes. But there are also other problems when sending a living, breathing crew into space.

The vast distances of space are one problem for a probe. They are another thing entirely for people to travel. At their closest possible points when orbiting the sun, Mars is 36 million miles (54.6 million km) from Earth. At their farthest, they are almost 250 million miles (401 million km) apart. By comparison, the moon is only approximately 240,000 miles (384,400 km) away. Even taking the shorter trip to the red planet, there are many challenges. One is the time required. Space probes can take years to reach their final destinations, and scientists think it would take six months to one year to reach Mars. A journey to Neptune would take eleven years! Imagine how long it would take us to reach one of the new exoplanets!

For a trip to Mars, we would need larger spaceships that can carry not only a larger crew but also all of the equipment they would need. A large craft needs larger launch equipment as well. Then there are landing systems to be built on Mars itself. We would probably need to build a space station in the planet's orbit to use as a landing base, and we'd need ways to protect astronauts from the heavy radiation.

The lack of gravity and the exposure to radiation in space mean that astronauts face possible health problems, including bone and muscle loss. The gravity issue is something already faced by astronauts on the International Space Station. They have to exercise for two and a half hours each day and take special supplements to help prevent bone loss. The crew on any long space mission will also need enough food and water for the journey. But that adds more weight to craft, unless there are efficient ways to produce food on a long space voyage. Another challenge is finding safe ways to recycle and reuse water.

Those are problems facing travel just within our solar system. Now think about travel between our solar system and other stars. In chapter 4, we discussed the Kepler space telescope's discovery of twenty-one planets that exist in the "habitable zone" of their stars. The closest of these is thirteen light years away. With our current technology, spacecraft or probes can't travel very fast relative to the distances that need to be covered to move between planets. Albert Einstein theorized that the fastest anything can travel is the speed of light. The speed of light is 186,000 miles per second (299,792 km per second). Even traveling at that astounding speed, it would take a probe or spacecraft thirteen years to reach the nearest habitable zone world. Scientists are working on developing ways to travel faster than the limit set by Einstein's theories. Researchers think that, under some conditions, neutrinos, tiny particles with almost no mass and no positive or negative charge, can travel faster than the speed of light.

If the researchers are right, scientists will need to re-examine many of the basic concepts of our modern understanding of space travel. It may also lead to the development of faster-than-light travel. It will change the way we look at travel within our solar system and beyond.

The huge distances to be traveled are not the only obstacle to space exploration. When a manned space craft is sent to Mars, its crew will face many challenges. NASA's plan is not to do the same kind of missions to Mars that it did to the moon. For the moon missions, the plan was to visit, take a few soil samples, and return to Earth. The goal for Mars is to have missions with astronauts on the planet's surface for up to one year, perhaps longer. That means providing food, water, and breathable air for two years during the mission

# Could There Be Alien Life in the Universe?

As the known universe grows and more planets are discovered, a common question is whether there might be other forms of life. Neil deGrasse Tyson is a physicist who studies space. He says that, even if there is no other life in our own solar system, there is probably life somewhere in the universe. We are considered carbon-based life forms. Life on Earth is based mainly around hydrogen, oxygen, and carbon. These are also the three most common elements in the universe. Therefore, Tyson thinks is very likely that another planet or moon has living creatures composed of the same elements.

People have often wondered about life on Mars. Others have thought that Saturn's largest moon Titan could contain some form of life, although it would be of a type able to survive in a rich methane atmosphere.

The Kepler space telescope has found at least 2,325 new exoplanets in its exploration. In 2014, scientists announced that one of these was a similar size to Earth, and showed indications of having water and an inhabitable atmosphere. The planet, named Kepler-186f, is about 490 light years from Earth. In 2015, researchers announced that another eight of the Kepler planets could also be capable of supporting life.

Just because there may be planets out there that can and do support life doesn't mean that we should expect them to look like us. A life form can be the simplest organism, a plant, an insect … any type of imaginable creature. Just as the planets in our solar system and beyond are all different, so should we expect life on those planets to be different.

(remember the six-month travel time each way). It also means creating a system that can support such missions.

Some of the research needed to make a Mars mission happen is already being done on the International Space Station. Scientists there are experimenting with the use of 3D printers to create tools for work in space. Instead of taking heavy specialized tool kits with them into space, they could take reusable powder resin that can be used to make the tool. Afterward, they can recycle the material for another 3D printing project. Taking this idea one step further, scientists are using data received from Martian probes about the content of Martian soil and rock. They wonder if it might be possible to create 3D printers that can use those elements on a large scale to print building materials for use on the planet's surface for living quarters and other structures.

Other NASA and Mars research is being carried out in South America. The environment of Chile's Atacama Desert is similar to that found on Mars. Scientists are replicating the Martian atmosphere there to see if it is possible to grow potatoes. Potatoes might be a valuable and nutritious food source on any manned mission to the red planet.

Another technology being developed by NASA scientists that will be vital to the exploration of Mars and beyond is Solar Electric Propulsion, or SEP. SEP works by using solar-generated electricity to remove electrons from gases. Removing the electrons will create ions. The ions can then be forced out of the spacecraft, creating thrust. This kind of system would not generate nearly enough thrust to launch a spacecraft from a planet's surface. But it could be used to slowly push heavy, unmanned payloads to Mars. When the astronauts arrive, many of the supplies they need would already be there waiting for them.

These are just a few examples of the technologies scientists believe will be crucial to manned exploration of other planets and moons within our solar system.

Even with technological advances, there are still some challenges that we do not often consider. One example is space junk. When a satellite stops working, we don't have any way to get it back, and it doesn't fall down to Earth. It simply stays in space as space junk. Now think of all the satellites circling Earth. There are satellites for communications, weather, and research. Then there are pieces of rock, parts that have broken off of manmade satellites, and more. That's a lot of stuff floating around. Scientists estimate that there are as many as 17,000 objects, bigger than a softball, circling Earth. If we include smaller objects, there could be as many as 500,000. Imagine driving a car while pieces of rock fly toward you. Now imagine the same thing in space! Researchers have suggested that all future satellites have special sails or boosters attached. This would mean that, when they are no longer useful, they can redirect toward Earth and burn up as they reenter the atmosphere.

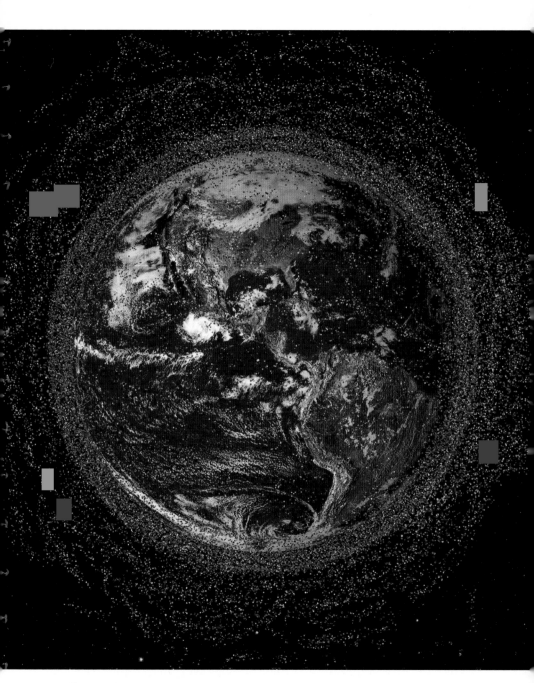

Thousands of pieces of space junk orbit Earth.

Otherwise, traveling through space may prove to be a very risky journey.

## SPACE TECHNOLOGY HERE ON EARTH

Exploring our universe has not just taught us about the planets. It has also benefitted our lives here on Earth. Lots of new technologies from the space program have been adapted for our everyday lives, and the results are too many to mention.

The first satellite, *Sputnik 1*, was launched in 1957. This was soon followed by the first communications satellites, a joint project between NASA and several corporations, which were launched in 1962. In our modern world, we rely on satellites for all sorts of everyday services. They help us make telephone calls around the world, and they send signals that go to our television sets. They also help to make sure we don't get lost. The Global Positioning System (GPS) grew out of satellite programs that were created to help the navy and air force. Now most of us have GPS in our cars and on our mobile phones, ensuring that we can always find our way when we are lost. GPS is also helping to warn us of natural disasters. A project in California has combined GPS monitors with moisture sensors. They allow weather forecasters in the area to predict heavy rains and issue warnings about possible flooding.

Technology adapted from NASA science is also helping to keep us healthy. Scientists created tools that use infrared technology to measure the temperature of stars and planets. The same method is used in modern ear thermometers, measuring heat energy from the eardrum and allowing for faster results than an oral thermometer. Scientists also use infrared imaging to help create visual data about planets and objects in space. That same imaging technology is regularly used by doctors to do many different tasks, from finding the tiniest of blood vessels to diagnosing brain injuries. Two other medical imaging procedures, CAT scans and MRIs, are the result of digital signal processes used on the Apollo missions. Since NASA needs to constantly monitor the health of their astronauts, hospitals now have more advanced monitoring equipment in intensive care units. The company that created systems for monitoring astronauts in space introduced advanced intensive care and critical care unit monitoring systems in the 1960s. As technology improved, they were able to incorporate digital microprocessors. Later came touchscreen controls, the ability to communicate the data with other computer systems, and remote monitoring. Even firefighters have benefitted from these technologies—they were adapted to create lighter-weight breathing apparatuses.

Earlier, we mentioned the problem of bone loss that results from long periods of time in a gravity-less environment. This is why the astronauts on the International

Space Station have to exercise for a few hours each day. Studies found that exercise alone did not help to prevent all bone loss, which is why the astronauts also have to take special nutritional supplements. Osteoporosis, a condition where a person's bones become weak and brittle, is a problem for many elderly people. Over time, it can cause serious problems. If an elderly person with osteoporosis falls, for example, their bones will break much more easily, and they can be difficult to mend. There are some drugs that can be used, not to cure the disease but to slow the rate of bone loss. However, studies that were done to help astronauts have led to several new treatment drugs. Hopefully, this might lead to the development of more drugs that will help both astronauts and people on Earth.

Space technology has even shaped automobile tires. In 1976, a new fiber was created for use in the parachutes that would land the Viking probes on Mars. The fiber needed to be incredibly strong but not too heavy—the resulting innovation is five times stronger than steel. After it was designed, the creators realized that it could produce a new tire that would last longer. Other special fabrics created to make spacesuits more comfortable are used to make swimsuits for Olympic athletes and even in special roof material on some buildings.

Space food might sound strange, but some food products are the result of researchers trying to find ways to make food last longer on voyages into space. During the Apollo missions, scientists needed to find ways to store food that would keep its nutritional value and make it easy to transport. Freeze-dried foods are cooked, frozen slowly, and then slowly reheated in a vacuum to remove ice crystals. The food keeps its nutritional value but weighs much less than the original packaged meal. Freeze-dried food can easily be stored and lasts a long time. It is perfect for camping and for use in meal-delivery programs. In the 1980s, experiments tested whether algae could clean water and recycle air on spacecraft, and perhaps be used as a food source. During the experiments, scientists found that they could produce a special nutrient that is now found in many popular baby formulas.

Perhaps one of the most interesting ways in which space technology has helped us on Earth is with our knowledge of global warming and climate change. In the early days of NASA's space exploration, researchers focused on Mars and Venus. As the nearest planets to Earth, it seemed possible that they might have similar environments and could be capable of supporting life. Instead, the Mariner missions discovered that Venus's atmosphere contained three hundred times more carbon dioxide than the atmosphere on Earth. The planet also had a super-hot surface temperature. Venus was our introduction to what we now call the greenhouse effect. This came at the same time that scientists on

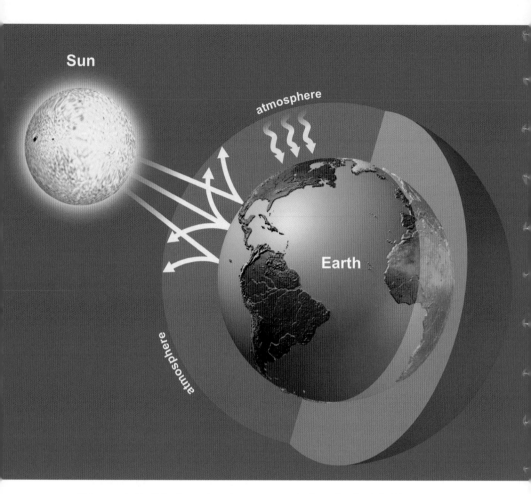

The gases in Earth's atmosphere keep us warm by trapping heat, but too many greenhouse gases cause global warming.

Earth were starting to notice important changes in our climate. They had always believed that such changes took thousands of years to occur. Recent discoveries showed that some changes had been very recent and very quick, taking just a few decades. This meant that climates could change dramatically in our lifetime. Greenhouse gases were becoming trapped in our own atmosphere. The discoveries on Venus made scientists curious as to whether something similar and so extreme could happen on Earth.

NASA didn't just help us to see the risks of the greenhouse effect by providing data about Venus. Satellites and imaging systems have enabled us to track climate change as it happens around the globe. Instruments on these satellites now chart temperatures, weather patterns, and more. All of that data is sent back to Earth to help researchers understand how fast change is happening and what we might do to slow it. One mission showed us that ice sheets in Antarctica and other frozen areas are melting more quickly than previously thought. Another has been able to show us the hole in the ozone layer.

NASA exploration to the other terrestrial planets showed us how serious the greenhouse effect could be on climate change. Now, NASA, the ESA, and other space agencies help us to monitor changes on our own planet. Their technological advances have also helped to improve our health and to make us safer. With new inventions and developments happening all the time, who knows what will come next?

Although some of these advances seem very complicated, it is important to remember that they all have their roots in something very simple that happened hundreds of years ago. People looked up into the sky and wondered about the things that glowed and twinkled. That led to them drawing maps and discovering stars and planets. Then came the next generations of curious people who looked at the maps and planets and wondered how they could learn more. Each generation of scientists has wanted to learn more and to build upon what others have discovered. In just a few hundred years, we have gone from a man looking at the sky through a newly invented telescope to sending probes far beyond the distances that his telescope could ever see or imagine.

# Glossary

**astronomical unit (AU)**  A unit of length equal to the distance between Earth and the sun, used as a way of describing other distances in space.

**astronomy**  The study of the stars and the planets.

**atmosphere**  The mass of air or gases that surrounds a planet.

**ellipse**  An oval shape. The paths of the planets around the sun are all ellipse-shaped.

**exoplanet**  A planet that orbits a star other than our solar system's sun.

**galaxy**  A system of stars and dust that are all held together by gravity. Galaxies come in different shapes, such as a spiral galaxy or an elliptical galaxy.

**gas giant**  The larger planets at the edge of the solar system that are made mostly of gases and have a mass much larger than that of Earth.

**geocentric** Having Earth at its center. People used to believe that our universe was geocentric and that the planets and sun revolved around Earth.

**gravity** A force that pulls one object to another.

**heliocentric** Having the sun at its center. Aristarchus and Copernicus both believed that our solar system was heliocentric, but Galileo and Kepler were the first to prove it.

**moon** A natural satellite that orbits a planet. Earth has one moon, while some planets have many. Moons that orbit other planets in our solar system often have names, for example, Ganymede (Jupiter) and Titan (Saturn).

**orbit** The path taken by one body as it travels around another body.

**planet** A body that follows a path around a sun and which is also large enough to have its own gravitational force.

**probe** A device sent into space to gather information and send the data back to Earth.

**satellite** Any object that moves around a planet. A satellite can be natural, like a moon or meteor fragments, or it can be manmade, like those that orbit Earth for communication.

**solar system** The sun and the planets and other objects that revolve around it.

**spectroscope** A tool that measures the properties of light. Astronomers use a spectroscope to study stars.

**sun** A star with planets that orbit it. The central object in our solar system.

**telescope** A tool that uses lenses or mirrors to see objects that are far away.

**terrestrial planet** A planet made mostly of rock. Earth, Mars, Mercury, and Venus are the terrestrial planets in our solar system.

# Further Information

## Books

Carson, Mary Kay. *Beyond the Solar System: Exploring Galaxies, Black Holes, Alien Planets, and More.* Chicago: Chicago Review Press, 2013.

Haugen, David M. *Jupiter.* San Diego, CA: KidHaven Press, 2002.

——. *Eyes on the Sky – Mars.* San Diego, CA: KidHaven Press, 2002.

## Websites

**Galileo's Telescope**
http://brunelleschi.imss.fi.it/telescopiogalileo/index.html
Galileo's Telescope is an online exhibition dedicated to the history of the astronomer and his telescopes.

**Imagine the Universe**
http://imagine.gsfc.nasa.gov
Imagine the Universe is a NASA-operated learning site for children aged fourteen and older.

**Solar System Scope**

http://www.solarsystemscope.com

Solar System Scope is an online interactive computer model showing the movement of the planets within our solar system and maps of the stars.

**StarChild**

http://starchild.gsfc.nasa.gov/docs/StarChild/StarChild.html

StarChild is a NASA-operated site to teach young learners about astronomy.

**Windows to the Universe**

http://www.windows2universe.org

The Windows to the Universe site is compiled by the National Earth Science Teachers Association, with information for students of all ages.

# Bibliography

Ashworth, Stephen. "Settlement of Mars: Is It Possible?" *SpaceFlight.* 58 (2016), 136–137.

Bakich, Michael E. "Voyager's 'New' Solar System." *Astronomy,* Jan. 2013, 30–35.

Fradin, Dennis Brindell. *Nicolaus Copernicus: The Earth is a Planet.* New York: Mondo Publishing, 2003.

Loewen, Nancy. *Farthest from the Sun: The Planet Neptune.* Minneapolis: Picture Window Books, 2008.

NASA. *Spinoff 2016.* NASA Headquarters, 2016. https://spinoff.nasa.gov/Spinoff2016/.

Reddy, Francis. "Our Solar System: Realms of Fire and Ice." *Astronomy,* Dec. 2015, 24–29.

Riebeek, Holli. "Planetary Motion: The History of an Idea That Launched the Scientific Revolution." *Earth Observatory.* July 7, 2009. http://earthobservatory.nasa. gov/Features/OrbitsHistory/page1.php.

Scott, Elaine. *When Is a Planet Not a Planet?: The Story of Pluto*. New York: Clarion Books, 2007.

Szocik, Konrad. "Unseen Challenges in a Mars Colony." *SpaceFlight*, 58 (2016), 20–23.

Wall, Mike. "What the Next 50 Years Hold for Human Spaceflight." Space.com. Apr. 12, 2011. http://www.space.com/11364-human-space-exploration-future-50-years-spaceflight.html.

# Index

# About the Author

**Fiona Young-Brown** lives in Kentucky, where she works as a freelance writer and book author. Young-Brown has written several books about the atomic age; she is the author of *Nuclear Fusion and Fission,* and has written a history of the Paducah Gaseous Diffusion Plant and its role through the Manhattan Project and beyond. She is also the author of three Kentucky history books, including *A Culinary History of Kentucky: Burgoo, Beer Cheese, & Goetta* and *Wicked Lexington, Kentucky.* Originally from England, Young-Brown enjoys travel, cooking, and researching history.